Table of Contents

Introduction

Life on Earth, as you know it, would be impossible without the humble fungi. In the beginning, fungi played an essential role in the development of our oxygen-rich atmosphere by mining phosphorous from the rocks and transferring it to plants to power photosynthesis. So, without fungi, your life as a human wouldn't be possible.

Also, fungi decompose practically everything that dies or decays. Without fungi, death would engulf the Earth, and make it virtually uninhabitable for you and every other living organism.

And Fungi impact your life significantly in ways you're likely unaware of, and you probably barely notice.

Fungi and Your Food

You may not know it, but fungi figure prominently in your diet. Mushrooms are the fleshy, spore-producing, fruiting body of fungi. Typically, mushrooms grow above ground and are but a minute portion of the larger organism that grows below ground, weaving its way through the soil and among the roots of plants.

No doubt you already know you can eat mushrooms and you should since they have a plethora of health benefits.

Morels, shiitake, chanterelles, and truffles are considered delicacies.But mushrooms aren't the only way fungi appear in your diet.Molds of the genus Penicillium ripen many kinds of cheese.

Fungi also ferment the grains and fruit to produce the beer and wine you drink, and they provide the wild yeast for bread.

Saccharomyces cerevisiae, also known as baker's yeast, is an essential ingredient in natural sourdough bread making, a food that's been a staple of human life for thousands of years.

Fungi and Your Health

Mushrooms fight cancer

A study in the Journal of Experimental Biology and Medicine found that all the common mushroom varieties reduced breast cancer cells by a whopping 33 percent. But breast cancer isn't the only type of cancer mushrooms help. Studies on prostate and stomach cancer show similar results.

They're immune-boosting and high in vitamins
Beta-glucan and lentinan are two properties found in mushrooms that give your immune system a much-needed boost. Plus, they're high in crucial vitamins — many mushroom varieties contain high levels of vitamin D, and crimini mushrooms carry lots of B12, which makes them an excellent choice for vegetarians since B12 is most common in animal products.

Fungi as Medicine

Red yeast rice is the earliest medicinal use of fungi on record.China developed it around 800 AD.Cultivating Monascus purpura (yeast) in rice produces a pharmaceutically active mixture of compounds.

Now, millions of patients with life-threatening diseases are treated each year with medicines made from fungi. The medicinal value of fungal metabolites is a knowledge that's centuries old.

Perhaps the most potent yet controversial fungal medicine is psilocybin mushrooms, medicinal properties have also been used for centuries.

In his book, "How to Change Your Mind: What the New Science of Psychedelics Teaches Us About Consciousness, Dying, Addiction, Depression, and Transcendence," Michael Pollan delves deep into the history of these drugs.

Pollan explains that psychedelics were once legal and used successfully in the US to treat mental disorders, including anxiety, depression, and addiction.According to Pollan, "For most of the 1950s and early 1960s, many in the psychiatric establishment regarded LSD and psilocybin as miracle drugs."

How They Work
Hallucinogens alter your perception, mood, and a slew of other mental processes by working their magic on your brain's cortex. The drugs activate specific receptors called 5-HT2A receptors (2ARs) that are typically triggered by serotonin.

This cascade of neurobiological changes to your brain helps you to experience a renewed wonder at everyday things. You'll have greater self-awareness. Your senses will be more acute so that colors appear more vibrant and sound, taste, and smell more intense. And you'll remain focused on the present.

The positive effects remain long after the drugs have left the building. Participants reported a significant reduction in anxiety and depression after just one use.

They also mentioned experiencing a "spiritual awakening," which was responsible for a permanent shift in their consciousness. Afterward, participants said it was easier to stay focused on the present, and they had a greater awareness of the interconnectedness of all things.

So, if you suffer from any of the aforementioned mental diseases, or you want to experience spiritual enlightenment and quiet the constant chatter in your mind, psilocybin mushrooms may be for you. And you may be wondering how to cultivate them.

Grow them

So, now that you know the extensive benefits of fungi and their mushrooms, are you ready to grow some? The following technique works for most types of mushrooms, but the focus of this article is on psilocybin cultivation.

Currently, it's illegal to cultivate psilocybin mushrooms in most countries. But, right now, medical researchers are working diligently to prove the therapeutic efficacy of psychedelic drugs like psilocybin, and they'll likely be legal soon. So, you can learn the process for when they become legal. Because you, of course, wouldn't dream of breaking the law, right?

At this point, you're probably wondering how long this process takes. That's a terrific question. Here's an approximate timeline:

- Spore inoculation to spore germination — within a week
- Spore germination to complete colonization of the cake — about 2 to 4 weeks.
- Start of fruiting cycle — approx two weeks.

- After two weeks or so, the cakes will begin to turn blue, and no more mushrooms will form.
- All in all, the process takes from 4–6 weeks from spore inoculation to fruiting.

Here's what you'll need:

Phase one —
- 10 Sterilized inoculation jars with a substrate. Or one jar for each cc in your syringe. You can also make inoculation jars with wide-mouth mason jars and brown rice flour or another substrate. But, you'll need to follow an intense sterilization process.
  Latex gloves
- Paper towels
- A face mask
- Rubbing alcohol

A syringe of mushroom spores (spore syringes are available on the internet. There are some states like California, Oregon, and Georgia to which most places won't ship. However, I did find one reliable source for those as well.

Hypodermic needles that are the correct size for your syringe. (if your syringe didn't come with them.

- A lighter
- A can of disinfectant spray (like Lysol)
- Phase two —
- A spray bottle
- A growing chamber — i.e., clear plastic tub with a lid
- Drill four or five 1/2 inch holes on either side of your growing box so air can circulate.
- A spot that receives plenty of indirect sunlight
- Temperature and humidity gauge
- Vermiculite (Some growers suggest Perlite. There is a difference between the two.)

There are four crucial aspects you'll need to get right to reap a reward for your efforts, and they are:

- Hygiene

- Humidity

- Light

- Temperature

You'll learn about each of these as we go through the steps. So, here goes:

Phase One

Phase one of your cultivation is where you'll create what's known as a birthing cake. A birthing cake is when mycelium has fully colonized your jar and wound around the substrate. When you turn it out of the mason jar, it will hold together like a cake and sprout mushrooms.

Step One: Sterilize

Enemy number one in mushroom cultivation is harmful bacteria hijacking your inoculation jars. That's why you're going to take the following steps to sterilize the jars and the surrounding environment.You're trying to keep minuscule microbes from creating murderous mayhem on your spores and multiplying in your jars.

Choose a small room in your house, like a bathroom that you can use as your secret laboratory (prep space).

Gather all the items on the phase one portion of your list. Don your face mask, enter the room and close the door.

Spray the room down reasonably well with the disinfectant spray. Then put on your gloves.

Wipe your jars off with rubbing alcohol using paper towels.Pay special attention to the top of the jar.

Step Two — Inoculate
Use your lighter and heat the metal portion of your hypodermic needle until it glows red. Typically hypodermic needles come pre-sterilized, so this is merely a precaution.

After you sterilize the needle, don't lay it down, continue to hold it until the needle cools down.

Shake your syringe to distribute the spores evenly. Insert the needle into the port and inject one cc into the jar.

Repeat with the remaining jars, sterilize your needle each time.

Step Three — Wait

After injection, place your jars in a cardboard box, close the lid, and put it in a dark, warm place. You'll want a steady temp of 80 to 85 degrees Fahrenheit. I know it's exciting, but try not to check your jars for five days. They need the dark.

After five days or so, a fuzzy, white substance will start to form in your jars. When this happens, jump up and down and perform a joyful, happy dance because this is a good sign.

The white substance you see is mycelium. Mycelium is the vegetative part of the fungus, similar to the roots of a plant. And the mushroom is like the flower on the plant.

Let the mycelium grow for approximately 15 days. Once your jars are 100-percent colonized by mycelium, wait a week then proceed to phase two.

Phase Two

Now it's time to remove the birthing cakes from their jars. Over the next month, they'll sprout mushrooms — hopefully, a whole plethora of them.

First, gather your jars and all the items on the list for phase two.

Step One — Prepare the chamber

Create a layer of vermiculite or Pearlite on the bottom of your growing chamber and moisten it thoroughly with your spray bottle. The vermiculite is there to help your growing chamber maintain humidity, and you will need to re-wet it periodically.

Step Two — Birth your mycelium cakes

Put on clean gloves or wash your hands — thoroughly.

Loosen the lids of your jars. Discard the band, but keep on the flat top.

Bang a jar against your hand to release the cake and let the cake slowly slide, lid side down, from the jar into the bed of vermiculite. (It may take a bit of banging and shaking to get the cake out of the jar. That's ok. Just be gentle and touch the cake as little as possible).

Repeat the process with each jar, but make sure you leave enough room between each cake, so there's plenty of room for mushrooms to sprout without crowding each other.

You may see little mushroom sprouts already forming. And that's a good thing.

Step Three
Using a delicate mist setting on your spray bottle, lightly mist the cakes, but don't spray them so much that water puddles on the cakes.

Step Four
Put the lid on your growing chamber and put it where it will receive indirect sunlight. The room should be well ventilated.

Maintenance
For the next month, mist your mushroom twice a day.Keep an eye on your humidity/temperature

gauge.Ideally, you want to maintain a temperature in the mid to low 70's and humidity of 35-percent.

Harvesting

When your mushrooms are ready for harvest, snap them off the birthing cake at the base of their stems and place them in an airtight container in your refrigerator. The cakes will only produce once, so discard them or use them in your yard as compost.

Yield, Storage, and Dosage

Your Yield

The primary image in this article is one of a fully ripe birthing cake that's ready for harvest. As you can see, one cake can yield plenty of mushrooms. I recommend ten jars because that's how many jars most syringes will innoculate.

Ten jars yield ten birthing cakes, which will produce more than a lifetimes supply for most people. You can start with fewer jars, which means you'll have leftover spores. Spores stay viable for eight months to one year, but dried mushrooms last far longer.

Storage

Mushrooms stay fresh for 3–15 days. Keep them in the fridge as you would any mushroom. After that, dry them and place them in an airtight container. Then place the container in a cool, dark place.

Dose

There is no set dosage for psilocybin mushrooms, so your dose depends on your size, sensitivity level, and the effect you desire. And it depends on the strength of the mushrooms.One mushroom can pack a punch, so start slow. You can't un-eat them if you take too much, but you can take more during your psychedelic journey. Just remember it can take up to an hour before you feel the effects.

Your set and setting are just as crucial as the dose you take, and there are steps you can take to ensure a positive experience.

A Final Word

Just like everything else in life, there are a gazillion methods for growing mushrooms. After you've grown a batch or two, you can debate all the daunting details of the perfect fungus growing process with experienced, enthusiastic experts who will, no doubt, make comments on this article. But if you're a beginner, this is a simple method you can wrap your brain around.

Do the number of steps feel a bit daunting? If so, re-read the steps until you can picture the entire process. Once you're familiar with the steps, they'll seem simple.

Lastly, don't focus on the result; enjoy the entire process. To grow anything is a privilege. But to cultivate a substance that can heal your mind and soul and transform your consciousness without adverse side effects is the mystery and magic of nature, and it deserves your appreciation.

How To Grow Psilocybin Mushrooms

[3-(2-Dimethylaminoethyl)-1H-indol-4-yl] dihydrogen phosphate

More and more people are growing psilocybin mushrooms at home. As well as providing a reliable, year-round supply, home cultivation eliminates the risk of misidentifying mushrooms in the wild. For many growers, it's also a fun, low-cost hobby.

If you don't know how to grow mushrooms at home, you may be tempted to start with a psilocybin mushroom grow kit. These ready-to-use packs contain a living mycelium substrate (the material underlying mushroom growth) that, in theory, you just need to keep humid.

In reality, you're better off starting from scratch.Making your own substrate is not only more consistent but, if you do it right, it should be less prone to contamination as well. There's also not a huge difference in price and you'll end up learning a lot more.

BACKGROUND

This guide is based on Robert "Psylocybe Fanaticus" McPherson's eponymous PF Tek—the method that revolutionized growing mushrooms indoors. McPherson's key innovation was to add vermiculite to a grain-based substrate (as opposed to using grain alone), giving the mycelium more space to grow and mimicking natural conditions. Although his method is a little more labor-intensive than others, often for a lower yield, its simplicity, low cost, and reliability makes it ideally suited to beginners. It also makes use of readily available materials and ingredients, many of which you may already have.

SPORE SYRINGES

The one thing you might have trouble getting is a good spore syringe. This will contain your magic mushroom spores and be used to "sow" them into the substrate. Some growers have reported issues of contamination, misidentified strains, and even syringes containing nothing but water. However, as long as you do your research and find a reputable supplier, you shouldn't have any problems.

In any case, after you've grown your first batch (or flush) of mushrooms, you can start filling syringes of your own.

WHAT VARIETY SHOULD I CHOOSE?

As you learn how to grow mushrooms indoors, you'll want to decide on a species and strain. Most suppliers offer a range to choose from, but the Psilocybe cubensis B+ and Golden Teacher mushrooms are among the most popular for beginners. While not as potent as some others, like Penis Envy, they're reportedly more forgiving of sub-optimal and changeable conditions.

WHAT YOU WILL NEED

INGREDIENTS

- Spore syringe, 10-12 cc
- Organic brown rice flour
- Vermiculite, medium/fine
- Drinking water
- EQUIPMENT
- 12 Shoulderless half-pint jars with lids (e.g. Ball or Kerr jelly or canning jars)
- Hammer and small nail
- Measuring cup
- Mixing bowl
- Strainer
- Heavy duty tin foil
- Large cooking pot with tight lid, for steaming
- Small towel (or approx. 10 paper towels)
- Micropore tape
- Clear plastic storage box, 50-115L
- Drill with ¼-inch drill bit
- Perlite
- Mist spray bottle

- HYGIENE SUPPLIES

- Rubbing alcohol

- Butane/propane torch lighter

- Surface disinfectant

- Air sanitizer

- Sterilized latex gloves (optional)

- Surgical mask (optional)

- Still air or glove box (optional)

- Optimize your microdosing efforts

LEARN HOW TO MICRODOSE

INSTRUCTIONS

The basic PF Tek method is pretty straightforward:
Prepare your substrate of brown rice flour, vermiculite,
and water, and divide it between sterile glass jars.
Introduce spores and wait for the mycelium to develop.
This is the network of filaments that will underpin your
mushroom growth. After 4-5 weeks, transfer your

colonized substrates, or "cakes", to a fruiting chamber and wait for your mushrooms to grow.

NOTE: Always ensure good hygiene before starting: spray an air sanitizer, thoroughly disinfect your equipment and surfaces, take a shower, brush your teeth, wear clean clothes, etc. You don't need a lot of space, but your environment should be as sterile as possible. Opportunistic bacteria and molds can proliferate in conditions for cultivating shrooms, so it's crucial to minimize the risk.

STEP 1: PREPARATION
1) Prepare jars:

With the hammer and nail (which should be wiped with alcohol to disinfect) punch four holes down through each of the lids, evenly spaced around their circumferences.

2) Prepare substrate:

For each jar, thoroughly combine ⅔ cup vermiculite and ¼ cup water in the mixing bowl.Drain excess water using the disinfected strainer.

Add ¼ cup brown rice flour per half-pint jar to the bowl and combine with the moist vermiculite.

3) Fill jars:

Being careful not to pack too tightly, fill the jars to within a half-inch of the rims.

Sterilize this top half-inch with rubbing alcohol

Top off your jars with a layer of dry vermiculite to insulate the substrate from contaminants.

4) Steam sterilize:

Tightly screw on the lids and cover the jars with tin foil. Secure the edges of the foil around the sides of the jars to prevent water and condensation getting through the holes.

Place the small towel (or paper towels) into the large cooking pot and arrange the jars on top, ensuring they don't touch the base.

Add tap water to a level halfway up the sides of the jars and bring to a slow boil, ensuring the jars remain upright.

Place the tight-fitting lid on the pot and leave to steam for 75-90 minutes. If the pot runs dry, replenish with hot tap water.

NOTE: Some growers prefer to use a pressure cooker set for 60 minutes at 15 PSI.

5) Allow to cool:

After steaming, leave the foil-covered jars in the pot for several hours or overnight. They need to be at room temperature before the next step.

STEP 2: INOCULATION

1) Sanitize and prepare syringe:

Use a lighter to heat the length of your syringe's needle until it glows red hot. Allow it to cool and wipe it with alcohol, taking care not to touch it with your hands.

Pull back the plunger a little and shake the syringe to evenly distribute the magic mushroom spores.

NOTE: If your spore syringe and needle require assembly before use, be extremely careful to avoid contamination in the process. Sterilized latex gloves and a surgical mask can help, but the surest way is to assemble the syringe inside a disinfected still air or glove box.

2) Inject spores:

Remove the foil from the first of your jars and insert the syringe as far as it will go through one of the holes.

With the needle touching the side of the jar, inject approximately ¼ cc of the spore solution (or slightly less if using a 10 cc syringe across 12 jars).

Repeat for the other three holes, wiping the needle with alcohol between each.

Cover the holes with micropore tape and set the jar aside, leaving the foil off.

Repeat the inoculation process for the remaining jars, sterilizing your needle with the lighter and then alcohol between each.

STEP 3: COLONIZATION
1) Wait for the mycelium:

Place your inoculated jars somewhere clean and out of the way. Avoid direct sunlight and temperatures outside 70-80 °F (room temperature).

White, fluffy-looking mycelium should start to appear between seven and 14 days, spreading outward from the inoculation sites.

NOTE: Watch out for any signs of contamination, including strange colors and smells, and dispose of any suspect jars immediately. Do this outside in a secure bag without unscrewing the lids. If you're unsure about whether a jar is contaminated, always err on the side of caution—even if the substrate is otherwise healthily colonized—as some contaminants are deadly for humans.

2) Consolidate:

After three to four weeks, if all goes well, you should have at least six successfully colonized jars. Leave for another seven days to allow the mycelium to strengthen its hold on the substrate.

STEP 4: PREPARING THE GROW CHAMBER
1) Make a shot gun fruiting chamber:

Take your plastic storage container and drill ¼-inch holes roughly two inches apart all over the sides, base, and lid. To avoid cracking, drill your holes from the inside out into a block of wood.

Set the box over four stable objects, arranged at the corners to allow air to flow underneath. You may also want to cover the surface under the box to protect it from moisture leakage.

NOTE: The shot gun fruiting chamber is far from the best design, but it's quick and easy to build and does the job well for beginners. Later, you may want to try out alternatives.

2) Add perlite:

Place your perlite into a strainer and run it under the cold tap to soak.

Allow it to drain until there are no drips left, then spread it over the base of your grow chamber.

Repeat for a layer of perlite roughly 4-5 inches deep.

STEP 5: FRUITING

1) "Birth" the colonized substrates (or "cakes"):

Open your jars and remove the dry vermiculite layer from each, taking care not to damage your substrates, or "cakes", in the process.

Upend each jar and tap down onto a disinfected surface to release the cakes intact.

2) Dunk the cakes:

Rinse the cakes one at a time under a cold tap to remove any loose vermiculite, again taking care not to damage them.

Fill your cooking pot, or another large container, with tepid water and place your cakes inside. Submerge them just beneath the surface with another pot or similar heavy item.

Leave the pot at room temperature for up to 24 hours for the cakes to rehydrate.

3) Roll the cakes:

Remove the cakes from the water and place them on a disinfected surface.

Fill your mixing bowl with dry vermiculite.

Roll your cakes one by one to fully coat them in vermiculite.This will help to keep in the moisture.

4) Transfer to grow chamber:

Cut a tin foil square for each of your cakes, large enough for them to sit on without touching the perlite.

Space these evenly inside the grow chamber.

Place your cakes on top and gently mist the chamber with the spray bottle.

Fan with the lid before closing.

5) Optimize and monitor coniditions:

Mist the chamber around four times a day to keep the humidity up, taking care not to soak your cakes with water.

Fan with the lid up to six times a day, especially after misting, to increase airflow.

NOTE: Some growers use fluorescent lighting set on a 12-hour cycle, but indirect or ambient lighting during the day is fine. Mycelium only needs a little light to determine where the open air is and where to put forth mushrooms.

STEP 6: HARVESTING
1) Watch for fruits:

Your mushrooms, or fruits, will appear as tiny white bumps before sprouting into "pins." After 5-12 days, they'll be ready to harvest.

2) Pick your fruits:

When ready, cut your mushrooms close to the cake to remove. Don't wait for them to reach the end of their growth, as they'll begin to lose potency as they mature.

NOTE: The best time to harvest mushrooms is right before the veil breaks. At this stage, they'll have light, conical-shaped caps and covered gills.

WHAT NEXT?

STORAGE

Psilocybin mushrooms tend to go bad within a few weeks in the fridge. So if you plan to use them for microdosing or you just want to save them for later, you'll need to think about storage. The most effective method for long-term storage is drying. This should keep them potent for two to three years as long as they're kept in a cool, dark, dry place. If they're stored in the freezer, they'll pretty much last indefinitely.

The lo-fi way to dry your mushrooms is to leave them out on a sheet of paper for a few days, perhaps in front of a fan. The problem with this method is they won't get "cracker dry." That is, they won't snap when you try to bend them, which means they'll still retain some moisture. They may also significantly diminish in potency, depending on how long you leave them out. Using a dehydrator is by far the most efficient method, but those can be expensive. A good alternative is to use a dessicant as follows:

- Air dry your mushrooms for 48 hours, ideally with a fan.
- Place a layer of dessicant into the base of an airtight container. Readily available dessicants include silica gel kitty litter and anhydrous calcium chloride, which you can purchase from hardware stores.
- Place a wire rack or similar set-up over the dessicant to keep your mushrooms from touching it.
- Arrange your mushrooms on the rack, ensuring they're not too close together, and seal the container.
- Wait for a few days, then test to see if they're cracker dry.
- Transfer to storage bags (e.g. ZipLoc, vacuum sealed) and place in the freezer.

REUSING THE SUBSTRATE

After your first flush, the same cakes can be re-used up to three times. Simply dry them out for a few days and repeat Step 5.2 (dunking). But don't roll them in the vermiculite; just place them back in the grow chamber and mist and fan as before. When you start to see contaminants (usually around the third re-use), drench the cakes with the mister spray and dispose of them outside in a secure bag.

MAKING SPORE SYRINGES

Filling your own psilocybin spore syringes is about as self-sufficient as it gets.

First, you'll need to take a spore print from a mature mushroom, i.e. one that's been allowed to grow until its cap has opened out and the edges are upturned. You should also notice an accumulation of dark purple deposits around the base.These are the magic mushroom spores.

To collect them, remove the cap with a flame-sterilized scalpel and place it gills down on a sterile paper sheet. Cover with a disinfected glass or jar to protect it from the air and leave for 24 hours. Keep the resulting spore print out of light in an airtight plastic bag.

To load a spore syringe, scrape some of the spore print into a sterile glass of distilled water. You can find this at auto supply stores. Then fill your syringe (which should also be sterile) and empty it back into the glass several times to evenly distribute the spores. Fill it a final time and place it inside an airtight plastic bag. Leave at room temperature for a few days to allow the spores to hydrate.You can then keep the syringe in the fridge until you're ready to use it.It should last at least two months.

ADAPTATIONS AND ALTERNATIVES
Numerous modifications have been made to the PF Tek method, both to increase yield and to make things easier. Different species also tend to produce better with different substrates and conditions.

The main alternative to the basic PF Tek is the monotub method, which involves spawning to bulk on coir (coconut fiber extract), manure, straw, or some other fresh and nutritious substrate. Eventually you may want to experiment with some of these other methods, but the PF Tek is a good introduction for now.

FAQs
How long does it take to grow magic mushrooms at home?

The time it takes for your mycelium-colonized substrate to put forth harvestable fruits depends on a number of factors. But the whole process of cultivating mushrooms should take between 1-2 months.

When to harvest shrooms?

You should be able to harvest your fruits 5-12 days after they first begin to sprout from the mushroom substrate.

The trick is to harvest them before the veil breaks, i.e before they fully mature and release their spores. In other words, the gills should still be covered. At this stage, your mushrooms should also have light, conical caps.

How to make a spore syringe?

We've included instructions for making a spore syringe above. You'll need a sterilized knife or scalpel, a sterile paper sheet, and a disinfected glass or jar to gather psilocybin spores from a mushroom allowed to mature. Add the mushroom spores to a glass of distilled water and load your sterile syringe from that. After leaving it at room temperature for a few days to hydrate, you can store it in the fridge for at least a couple of months.

How to grow mushrooms at home without spores?

Use a Psilocybe cubensis grow kit if you don't want to add the mushroom spores yourself. The typical cubensis grow kit comes with an already colonized substrate for growing mushrooms in a box. They're available for different cubensis varieties, as well as different species.

But magic mushroom grow kits are not without their critics.

What's wrong with using a magic mushroom grow kit?

Despite their seeming convenience, magic mushroom grow kits are widely seen as a waste of money. Even if they work out at roughly the same price as starting from scratch, their contents and quality are uncertain. They can also be more prone to contamination.

Going by user reports, they may not even work. At best, they yield inconsistent results. Aside from anything else, using a cubensis grow kit won't teach you how to cultivate magic mushrooms from scratch.

What is the best mushroom substrate?
Although tried and tested by generations of mushroom growers, the brown rice flour and vermiculite substrate may not be the best choice for everyone. It depends on your priorities. Brown rice flour is good for growing in bulk, but coir may be cheaper and easier to use. Then there's whole brown rice (not flour), which supposedly yields more potent fruits.

Pasteurized horse manure is another good option, since it's high in phosphorus, nitrogen, and potassium. And throwing spent coffee grounds into the mix (up to a quarter of the whole) could help speed up colonization.Of course, spent coffee grounds are economical too; the 99% of coffee biomass that doesn't end up in the cup is usually just thrown away.

Some growers say the best mushroom substrate is crammed full of nutritional diversity. However, too many nutrients from too many different sources can lead to contamination. As a beginner, you're better off keeping things simple–not to mention cheap enough for trial and error.

What's the difference between magic mushroom spawn and substrate?

As you learn more about growing mushrooms indoors, you're likely to see the terms 'spawn' and 'substrate' used seemingly interchangeably (or just incorrectly).

Put simply, your 'substrate' (the brown rice flour/vermiculite cakes in the PF Tek method) becomes 'spawn' if it's used to colonize a second, 'bulk substrate' (coir, manure, etc.) in the fruiting chamber.

If you're fruiting directly from the cakes, as directed by this guide, your mushroom substrate remains the 'substrate' even after removal from the jars.

What are the best Psilocybe cubensis strains?
As mentioned in the guide, some of the most popular P. cubensis strains (or varieties) for beginners are the B+ and Golden Teacher mushrooms. Experienced growers may prefer Penis Envy.

However, as with your choice of substrate, the best cubensis strain for you will depend on your priorities for cultivating mushrooms.See here and here for more information.

How to grow magic truffles?

Forget about growing mushrooms in a box; truffles are often grown in jars instead of a fruiting chamber. See this tek for details. Another key difference to the PF Tek as outlined above is the use of a boiled rye grain (aka rye berries) substrate.

Popular truffle varieties include P. mexicana and P. tampanensis, also known as 'philosopher's stones'.

Where can I find supplies for growing mushrooms?

One of the great things about the PF Tek method is that supplies are widely available. What you haven't already got lying around the house can be found at your local hardware store.

The only thing you'll need a specialist supplier for is your first load of psilocybin spores. The best way to find a reputable one is through forums.

How to grow Magic Mushrooms at home? (Pro's & Cons)

Growing at home is more accessible than ever! With the different cultivation methods available, it might be good to ask yourself: "which cultivation method fits me the best?". To help you answer this question, we made a pros and cons overview of each magic mushroom cultivation option. At the end you'll have clear vision on how you want grow magic mushrooms at home!

Grow magic mushrooms at home (pro's and cons)

Customers of The Magic Mushroom Shop have a great variety of options when it comes to cultivation methods. Simple and fast? Get a MycoMate Golden Teacher! Interested in starting from scratch? Try PF Tek! Or maybe something in between? Go for the MycoMate Kilo Kit! In this book, we will discuss 3 common cultivation methods:

- Mycelium grow kits
- Spores have already germinated to mycelium and colonized the substrate of the grow kit.

- These grow kits are easy to use, give quick results and come with clear instructions.

MycoMate or Freshroom XP?

MycoMate: classic and reliable, takes a little more energy and attention to cultivate, seems to last the longest.

FreshMushroom XP: the new popular grow kit in town, the easiest instructions available, great for busy people, has a fertile white coat around the substrate.

Pro's

- Clean and discreet
- Easy and perfect for beginners
- The fastest option for growing magic mushrooms at home

Con's

- Limited to one way of cultivation.

- Experienced cultivators will want more options to maximize and customize the cultivation process.

Growing magic mushrooms from scratch

Grow magic mushrooms from sporesThere are several steps to consider when you're starting from scratch, like producing the substrate, inoculation, incubation and cultivation (video instructions here). But it all starts with the spores!

In our store, psilocybe cubensis spores are available in 3 different varieties:

- Vials
- Syringes
- Prints

Pro's

- The cheapest option.
- Shelf life of spores are longer than grow kits.
- More flexibility and possibilities for maximizing and customizing the cultivation process.

- Spores are legal in most countries, for research purposes. And the same applies to the separate cultivation necessities.

Cons

- There's a small learning curve. It takes some time and effort to learn the process of making your own cake.

- Next to spores, you'll need to be familiar with the cultivation necessities that go along with the Magic Mushroom Tek of your choice.

- Starting from scratch takes more time than mycelium grow kits.

- The work environment must be 100% hygienic, any contamination will sabotage the whole process.

Grow Kits Without Mycelium

At the Magic Mushroom Shop we're very excited about these kits. Grow kits without a mycelium colonized substrate are flexible, discreet and expand the possibilities for cultivation. No mycelium or psilocybin, means that these kits are legal almost all around world.

Span bag kilo kitDelivered with an outstanding pre-produced substrate, these grow kits can save you time, while still giving you full control over the inoculation and incubation phase. This is the phase where you will bring the mycelium and psilocybin to life! Of course, there are detailed instructions on how this whole process works.

Next to magic mushrooms, you can also cultivate edible and medicinal mushrooms with a Kilo Kit or a Fast Fungi. Just as exciting is growing your own home made truffles with the Underground Kit.

Grow Kit Without Mycelium
Pro's

- Ultimately cheaper than Mycelium Grow Kits. The Kilo Kit may cost more but it'll also yield more.
- Shelf life of grow kits without mycelium are longer than Mycelium Grow Kits.

- Easier than starting from scratch.Also cleaner and faster.
- Spores are legal in most countries, for research purposes.And the same applies to the separate substrate.

Cons

- There's a small learning curve. It takes some time and effort to learn the process of inoculation and incubation.
- No control over the ingredients of the substrate.
- The work environment must be 100% hygienic, any contamination will sabotage the whole process.

www.ingramcontent.com/pod-product-compliance
Lightning Source LLC
Chambersburg PA
CBHW051402150726

48000CB00003B/1302